85 M

Dollar Tips

FOR

Financial Advisors

Maribeth Kuzmeski,
author of *Red Zone Marketing:
A Playbook for Winning All
The Business You Want*

85 Million

Dollar Tips

———

FOR

———

Financial Advisors

Acknowledgments

A special thank you to Celia Rocks and Melanie Springer, who have been instrumental in producing this book. Without their commitment to Red Zone Marketing, I would forever remain 100 yards from the end zone!

Maribeth Kuzmeski

Introduction

A Word From Maribeth Kuzmeski

Financial advisors have *a lot* of competition.

Think about it. There are hundreds of thousands of financial advisors and insurance agents. A seemingly unlimited drove of financial products. Thousands of mutual funds. And all of this boils down to one simple, disheartening fact: you are in serious peril of becoming a commodity.

Your only recourse is to prove that <u>you</u> are different. That <u>you</u> are *better*. That <u>you</u> offer your clients something above and beyond the services offered by your competitors. That <u>you</u>, better than anyone else, can help them manage the murky and confusing yet opportunity-filled world of investing and money management.

And that is precisely why I wrote this book.

My company, Red Zone Marketing, specializes in helping financial service companies set themselves apart from the crowd and, ultimately, win all the business they want. The information in this book—which is carefully packaged in 85 bite-sized, easy-to-understand marketing tips—reflects the advice I offer my clients every day.

As you read this book you will notice that, occasionally, I make references to football. That's because my business philosophy is based on the football-related analogy of helping my clients get into—and score from—the *Red Zone*.

If you're a football fan, you know that the *red zone*—that unmarked territory between the defending team's 20-yard line and the end zone—is the most critical and magnified part of the field. Often, it determines whether a team wins or loses a game. Likewise, in business, the *Red Zone* is that unmarked territory right before the sale closes where you either win or lose a client.

Of course, it's not necessary to be a football fan in order to benefit from this book. The tips stand alone quite nicely. I just wanted you to understand why you're going to see the occasional reference to goal posts or game plans!

I hope you will find the ideas in this book thought provoking, useful and above all, profitable. I don't expect you to implement all 85 of these marketing tips, by the way. Some will be appropriate for your company, others will not. That's okay. Marketing is an art, not a precise science.

However, I can make you two promises. Number one, these tips <u>work</u>. I *know* they work because I have seen the results that occur when my clients follow them faithfully and enthusiastically. Number two, these tips are <u>fun</u>.

Yes, you read that last sentence correctly. Marketing can be—and *should* be—exciting and enjoyable. If you don't see the fun in spreading the good news about your company and dreaming up creative ways to outscore the competition, you're not doing it right. Now is your chance to remedy that!

Here's my advice. Sit down, turn off your phone, and read this book cover to cover. You might even want to flag your favorites. Then, make a commitment to spend an hour each week doing the work necessary to implement the ones that really speak to you. You will be amazed at the transformation that takes place in your business.

And now, dear reader, I invite you to leap full force into the world of *Red Zone Marketing* . . . and get ready to score, again and again and again!

1

Get Your "Vision" Checked.

I'm not talking about a visit to your local optometrist. But since this is a book about marketing, you probably figured that out. When I say *vision*, I'm referring to your own mental image of what your business *should* be. The big picture. What will your financial services company look like in, say, ten years?

If you don't yet have a clear vision of your future, you're not alone. Most people don't. Unfortunately, that's why so many businesses fail—or at least fail to *thrive*. As Yogi Berra once said, "If you don't know where you're going, when you get there you'll be lost."

Before you read any further, take an hour (or a day, or a week, if you need it) to dream up—and commit to paper—your business vision. Make it as grand and glorious as you want...even if it's *so* grand and glorious you suspect you'll never attain it.

I realize this seems like a tall order—and it is. But the rest of the tips in this book won't do you much good if you don't know where you're headed.

2

Your Mission, Should You Choose To Accept It...

Now that you've conceived your vision, it's time to come back down to earth. It's time to write your mission statement! (I can hear the groans now, but this is a critical step in becoming a *Red Zone* marketer.)

If you're confused about the difference between a *vision* (last tip) and a *mission* (this tip), take a cue from Jeffrey Abrahams, author of *The Mission Statement Book*. He wrote, "A vision is something to be pursued, while a mission is something to be accomplished."

In short, decide what you'd like to accomplish—your reason for being in business—and sum it up in a few short & sweet sentences. If you need more guidance, consider AT&T's mission statement:

We aspire to be the most admired and valuable company in the world. Our goal is to enrich our customers' personal lives and to make their businesses more successful by bringing to market exciting and useful communications services, building shareowner value in the process.

Does that help you focus? Good! Now grab your pen (or your keyboard) and start writing.

Set Up Your Goal Posts.

Now, it's time to get specific and measurable goals. Football fan that I am, I like to call them "goal posts." A goal post is *not* a general statement like "I want more clients." *Of course* you want more clients! But stated so vaguely, it's nothing more than wishful thinking. A specific, measurable goal post might be "I want to increase my client base by 20% in the next 12 months."

If you currently have 30 clients, a 20 percent increase means adding six new clients during the coming year. But if you wait until the eleventh month to begin working toward that goal, you won't reach it. This is why you need *sub*-goal posts. For example: "I will add one new client every two months."

Once you've set up your goal posts and sub-goal posts, you'll have something to aim for. The rest of this book will give you some specific ideas on how to move toward these goal posts (i.e., into the *Red Zone* and on to the end zone).

Read on…the game's about to get really interesting!

4

Add an MVP to Your Team

Of course YOU are the Most Valuable Player on your team. Right? Well, what if you looked at yourself as the coach and general manager, not the running back? You are calling the plays and your employees are running them.

Why not add an MVP to your team that will give you the opportunity to sell more, with fewer headaches? Hire a New Business Coordinator (or "NBC" for short). Many financial advisors have found that such an individual pays for him/herself countless times over by freeing up their time and insuring that follow-up is being done.

The NBC joins you in every new business appointment…hears firsthand what needs to be done in order to transform a prospect into a client…schedules the follow-up appointments, prepares the paperwork, enters notes into the database, conducts research, and prepares first drafts of financial plans. He or she creates a relationship with the prospect by giving that person another point of contact in the office (besides you).

This extraordinary individual will help you where you need it the most. When someone is on top of every detail, you can do what you do best—sell, and be a great financial advisor.

5

Who Loves Ya Babe?

You are a great financial advisor. You know it and your clients know it. But your *staff* needs to know it, and believe it as well.

If your staff doesn't think that you are the best financial advisor in the world, consider letting them in on your little secret. You see, if they don't think you are super fantastic at what you do, how can they possibly transfer that information on to your prospective and current clients?

Let them know when you have received an industry or broker dealer award. Show them client notes and emails. Have them sit in on meetings so they can see firsthand how you change lives.

Your staff needs to believe. If they don't, won't or can't— find someone who does, will and can!

6

No Napping On the Job.

Don't rest on your laurels. When your marketing is working and you are reaching your goals, take advantage of the best time you have to step your marketing up a level (yes, do it when the going is good!). When you have momentum, ensure that it continues.

If you decide that business is great now and that no more marketing will be necessary, there is the possibility that sometime in the future your pipeline of prospects will run dry. Continue to communicate effectively with your clients, your prospects, and the community to cultivate and grow your client base for the long term.

7

Get All The MOTT.

Do you ever leave Money-On-The-Table (MOTT)? Far too many financial advisors miss opportunities the client presents. Before long you may be on to the next sale with another client and the opportunity is long forgotten.

You close the first sale with one product, but the client may also need long term care insurance or life insurance or may have investments that you are not managing. Record the MOTT opportunities in your database. Schedule follow-up calls, letters, and appointments to address MOTT. Pay attention to opportunities that can bring extra income to you. Don't let the details slip through the cracks. Get the MOTT *off* the table!

You Have Something
The Media Wants.

I'm going to let you in on a little secret. Newspapers, magazines and even radio and TV stations need lots of stories. What's more, they need them *fast*. And generally speaking, they don't have enough reporters to go out and find those stories. They rely on press releases—well-written, fact-filled, *newsworthy* ones—to fill up the empty spaces and the dead air time.

That's where you come in. Maybe you're offering a truly cutting-edge estate-planning seminar...or you've just been hired to manage the money of a major 401K...or you've come up with a can't-fail investment strategy guaranteed to make every client rich. (Okay, you can always dream!)

The point is, *something* about your company is interesting and relevant enough to be covered in the media. It's your job to figure out what that something is. Then, tell the media. This is called *public relations*, or *PR* for short. It's like advertising, but better—you don't have to pay for the space, and since it's presented as "news," it has more credibility. Honest.

9

Do Your Media Homework.

Okay, now that you have some great ideas for press releases, who are you going to send them to? Good question. The answer is pretty simple. Just ask yourself: *What media will reach my target audience; i.e., potential customers for my firm?* Once you have the answer, you're ready to start building your media list.

Your list should include four major types of outlets. One is *newspapers*, both big city, and, suburban—daily, weekly and monthly—plus wire services and syndicates. Another is *magazines*, both consumer and trade. Assuming that you're a financial advisor, examples might be *Registered Rep* and *Senior Market Advisor*. The other two categories are TV stations and networks, and radio stations and networks.

Once you've created your list, get copies of each publication and read them from cover to cover. Also, listen to targeted radio stations, concentrating on talk shows and news stories. Watch programs on your targeted TV outlets, paying particular attention to talk shows and feature stories with a local angle.

See what you're doing? You're figuring out what type of material the various media outlets want, so you can target your PR efforts accordingly. Simple, huh?

10

The Art of the Press Release.

Ahh, the heart-stopping terror of facing a blank sheet of paper! (or, since we're living in the Computer Age, a blank word-processing document). Writer's block doesn't have to de-rail your PR efforts, though. Just follow these simple tips:

- Be sure it reads like news. Avoid acronyms, jargon and self-promotional language. And don't start your release by writing that your organization "is [pleased] [happy] [honored] to announce, etc." Just write "has announced" and keep going.
- Include the name, address, and phone number of your organization, as well as the date, contact person for obtaining additional information, and release date.
- Write an eye-catching headline, then be brief and to the point. Put the key elements of your story in the opening paragraph. The easier you make a busy editor's job, the better.
- Have at least one other person proofread your copy for accuracy, spelling, grammar and punctuation. Also, keep a style manual handy. *The Chicago Manual of Style* and *The Associated Press Style Manual* are two of the most popular.

11

Learn What Editors Like...And What They Don't.

First, let me point out that your media list (discussed in Tip #9) should include the (accurately-spelled!) names of editors, reporters, columnists, station managers, talk show hosts, producers, etc. People do change jobs, so be sure that you update your list periodically.

When you call your contacts, keep your conversation well-focused and as brief as possible, introducing yourself and the organization you represent. Know what you're going to say before you call, including your main news angle and any alternate angles.

For future reference, find out when and how your media contacts want to be, well, *contacted*. Do they prefer e-mails, faxes, disks, etc.? Then, keep a record of all contacts, including date, time, subject matter and any follow-up you need to do.

One final caveat: *do not* send out a release and then immediately call editors with an annoying, high-pressure "sales pitch" aimed at getting them to run your story. If the story is newsworthy—and if there's enough print space or air time available—they'll use it. At any rate, the editor doesn't owe you anything...so don't be a pest.

12

Remember the Two Magic Words.

Mom was right. *Thank you* goes a long way in every situation. And when you're trying to build a long-term relationship with an editor, these two magic words can mean the difference between a splashy feature on your financial consulting firm and your news release being unceremoniously tossed into the "round file."

When a release you send is used, call the person responsible and say thank you. Better still, send a brief handwritten note. (Editors rarely get them, and they *will* remember your thoughtfulness in the future.)

A consistently friendly attitude will help ensure positive media relationships. Keep your door open to reporters; when they seek additional information, go the extra mile to provide it. And remember, as in every area of your life, your best credential is your integrity.

13

Keep 'Em Informed with an Organization Newsletter.

Since 1916, this form of communication has been a major marketing tool for American companies. Why? Simply put, an organization newsletter lets you deliver consistent messages about your products or services directly to a targeted audience of readers—be they clients, prospects, suppliers, shareholders, employees or others.

Newsletters build credibility and awareness of your organization in the crowded financial advisor marketplace, while stimulating good will and boosting opportunities for repeat sales.

Also, newsletters are flexible. Just like a football team uses a wide variety of running and passing plays in executing its game plan, you can use your newsletter in various ways: as a sales, advertising, PR, educational and/or promotional tool.

Why not start planning yours now? Find someone in your company who has the time and writing ability—and *commitment!*—to do a top-quality job. If that's impossible, be aware that there are many ad agencies, PR firms and other communications companies that will happily take the project off your hands.

The next two tips will give you some specific guidelines for great, readable newsletters.

14

Newsletter Know-How (Part I)

A few hints for producing a top-notch organizational newsletter…

- Aim for a "FOG Index" of 12 or less. The Index equates to the educational level needed to even comprehend written material (16 = college graduate). The most popular business publications average in the 11 range.
- Start small. If you're just beginning, stick to a maximum of four pages, which will give you enough space to convey your message effectively.
- Make a good first impression. Begin two or three articles on the front page and continue them on the inside. Strive for a "breaking news" look and feel.
- Establish credibility. Address hot, current issues within the financial industry. Use people outside your company to write articles. Also, writing in the "third person" is more believable than the first-person style many newsletters use.
- Be brief. In today's fast-food, sound-bite, instant-everything society, readers prefer more and shorter stories, rather than a few long articles.
- Variety is still the spice of life—and of newsletters. Unfortunately, many newsletters include only subject matter about the companies that produce them. Logical but boring. Aim for variety and include a column of bite-sized fillers— quotations, interesting events, comments from trade journals, etc.

15

Newsletter Know-How (Part II)

…and even <u>more</u> newsletter hints!

- Use pictures. They attract attention! Use pictures of your clients, your staff, and your events. Also, use pictures to illustrate your points.
- Use quotations. Well-chosen ones can enliven articles, illustrate points, change the pace, get attention, trigger emotion, and add humor. Not only can they reinforce your message, they can fill small "holes" that cause layout problems.
- Tickle the reader's funny bone. Anecdotes and quotations can be used effectively to get readers smiling. (Who says financial advisors don't have a sense of humor?) A humorous column shows that you don't take yourself too seriously.
- Stick to a schedule. Football practices and games don't get underway whenever everyone decides to just show up. Neither should your newsletter. Start with your targeted mailing dates and work backward, including deadline dates for every step in the process: copy submission, typesetting, printing, etc.
- Build in bounce-back. Make it easy for readers to contact you for extra copies, free offers, more information, etc. Include phone numbers with extensions, fax numbers and people's names, not just departments.
- Profread, proofred and proofread again! *Gotcha!*

16

Recycle Your Organization Newsletter.

No, I'm not talking about throwing it in the recycling bin or using it to line Tweety's birdcage. You probably think of each issue of your organization newsletter as a "one time" mailing to customers and employees. But you can use back issues in numerous ways. Hand them out at trade shows...send them to prospective customers as a part of a "get to know us" package...give them to editors who need "background" on your company...post them on your Web site. Bottom line? Hang on to those old newsletters. You never know when you might need them.

17

Forget Your Brochure – When Was The Last Time You Read One?

If you think brochures are the way to go to promote your business, consider the last time you read a brochure from cover to cover? *Really?*

You need a brochure only if you "think" you need one. Consider using a one-page information sheet that describes your highlights in easy-to-read bullet points, contains pictures of happy clients, and describes your business, your office, your staff and the services and solutions you provide.

A single sheet is easy to read—or to skim, as the case may be. And, don't forget to use your picture and/or a picture of your entire staff. A picture is worth a thousand words, and no matter what you look like, ultimately you are selling yourself…and you are who you are. So forget your camera-shy nature and flash them a smile!

18

Give Video Marketing a Try.

At first glance, financial planning doesn't evoke the most exciting visual imagery. But when you consider what your clients can buy with the money you help them save and create—say, grandkids playing in front of a charming beach cottage or a family hiking in the European countryside or a new luxury car zipping around curves—some compelling pictures spring to mind.

That's why video marketing is great for companies in your field. Via video, walk them through the process that clients go through when doing business with you. Video can convey the spectacular benefits your services offer clients far better than a static photo or words on paper. It hits people on an immediate, gut level. So why not create a spectacular sales video (DVD) and send it to your top prospects?

According to a study by the Wharton School of Business at the University of Pennsylvania, prospects that watch a marketing video make their buying decision 70 percent faster than those who only read a brochure. What's more, according to Technicolor Video Services, about 94 percent of the people who watch your video will pass it along to a friend or relative.

Pretty impressive statistics, huh?

19

Video On The Cheap?

Worried about the costs of producing a marketing video? Don't be. A bit of shopping around will help you find a good deal. Perhaps a small video production company in your area will charge considerably less than a large, full-service facility. Or you may be able to save money by contacting video students at your local college.

A word of warning, however: don't sacrifice quality in order to save a few pennies. The cost of producing a good marketing video is an investment in your company—one that will get you into, and through, the *Red Zone.* In other words, don't be *too* much of a Scrooge!

20

It's Time To Weave
Your Web Site.

To be accepted as a legitimate business today, it's virtually essential (no pun intended) that you have a presence on the Internet. Let me say it another way. If you present yourself as a successful firm, yet lack a Web site and use an e-mail address from one of the free providers, red flags go up—and they'll make your job of reaching the *Red Zone* much harder. (Red flags and *Red Zones* definitely don't mix!)

The Web can broaden your potential marketplace from your home city to the entire nation and even across international borders.

The Web makes it possible to house all your business marketing collateral online, eliminating or reducing the need for brochures and other marketing materials. (Think how much money you'll save on printing!)

The Web offers the capacity to project a favorable, positive corporate image easily and cost-effectively. In other words, if you're a financial services firm with one employee, you can look just as professional as one with 20.

Get the point? It's time to weave your Web site...don't wait another day!

21

Already Have A Web Site?
Get It Evaluated.

I almost didn't include this tip, but then I thought better of it. Know why? Because too many companies have a Web site that isn't helping them. Maybe it's outdated because your company has drastically changed. Maybe you slapped it together in five minutes back in 1996, just so you could say you had a Web presence. Or maybe it looks professional but simply isn't meeting your company's goals.

Here's my suggestion: ask someone you respect to evaluate your site. It could be a Web expert, preferably one with experience in the financial services industry. And/or it could be one or more of your most important customers. Just get outside feedback. It's hard to be objective about your own Web site— *especially* if you're the one who developed it! (Hey, you're only human.)

22

Don't Let Your Internet Home Collect Cobwebs.

Ever visited a corporate Web site only to find that absolutely *nothing* about it had changed since your *last* visit—a year earlier? Chances are, you were left with the impression of a stale, dusty, unimaginative company. Sure, maybe they were too darn busy to update their site. But you, the visitor, can't know that…and in marketing, perception is reality.

Now, apply this principle to your own Web site. Have you updated it lately? You should. As a financial advisor, you might write a regular column on current economic news and make it an integral part of your site. This will give clients and potential clients a reason to bookmark your Web site and visit it regularly.

Another (less work-intensive) tactic to consider is posting a link on your welcome page that takes visitors to your most recent press release. Alternately, at least once a week—even once a day—add a thought-provoking quote or bit of humor to your site. Anything to prevent repeat visitors from getting bored and going elsewhere!

23

Personalize Your Mass E-Mails.

Let's say you're offering a new service...or have some market news you'd like to share...or you've hired a new employee...or you've just been named Financial Advisor of the Year. Naturally, you want to share the big news, so you send out a mass e-mail to your database of 500 clients, prospects and business associates. Easy, huh?

Well, yes. E-mail can be a wonderful communication tool. Just don't address your *e*-nnouncement to "whom it may concern." (This is the true definition of spam!) Instead, invest in a database program that personalizes your e-mails. It's an easy thing to do, and it makes your message much more personal.

Oh, and by the way: when e-mailing a client in response to a question, put his or her name in the greeting—it's not hard to do and it makes the recipient feel special.

24

Try An E-Newsletter.

Back in Tips 13–16, I discussed the ins & outs of traditional corporate newsletters. Well, guess what? In the Internet Age, there's a great alternative that'll save you big bucks on printing, envelope stuffing and postage. That's right. I'm talking about the *e*-newsletter.

Monthly, bimonthly or quarterly e-mails filled with short segments of news from your company, suggestions for making clients' lives or jobs easier, valuable coupons, and notification of special events make a great marketing tool. Just be sure you put as much thought into your e-newsletter as you would a traditional direct mail campaign. If it seems thrown together—or worse, irrelevant—it'll only serve to annoy clients. And make sure you get clients and prospects to opt-in. Let them tell you if they want to receive your email newsletter.

Receiving regular, *useful* communications from you will keep your company uppermost in clients' minds—and will make them feel that they matter.

25

Use E-Mail to "Keep In Touch."

I'm going to talk a lot more about establishing a "Keep In Touch" (or KIT) Program later in this book. But since I'm on an e-mail tangent, I decided to bring up this subject now: you can use e-mail to keep yourself at the top of your clients' minds.

For instance, you might send e-greeting cards to your clients on their birthdays and on holidays. Or if you come across something you know a specific client would be interested in—say, a fascinating article about his industry or a link to a Web site about one of his hobbies—e-mail it to him with a "this made me think of you" note.

The beauty of e-mail is its immediacy and its casual, "off the cuff" nature. You want clients to know that you think of them and their wants and needs often—and any reminder of your devotion can only strengthen your business relationship.

26

Cherish Those Client Kudos.

Want to know your most valuable marketing asset? Truly delighted clients. Think about it. You can write (or hire someone to write) glowing ad copy. You can hire models to pose in ads touting their extravagant new lifestyles (thanks to your advice). You can develop the snazziest Web site ever. But not a single one of these tactics possesses the power of a simple, heartfelt, *honest* comment from a delighted client.

That's why, if you do happen to receive a card or letter from Mr. or Ms. Happy Investor raving about your financial wisdom and stellar service, *keep it*. Share it with your staff. Think about how you can get more. If a client takes the time and effort to write you a note about how happy they are, you must be doing a lot of things right. Congratulations.

Spontaneous expressions of gratitude and appreciation are scarcer than hen's teeth. What's more, they're valuable.

27

A Picture Says A Thousand Words.

If you're looking for some extra ways to show your potential clients about your firm and the experience they will get when working with you, try showing them through pictures. Pictures tell people a lot of positive things about your firm without you having to verbalize it.

Consider having pictures taken with you and each of your happy clients. You and smiling Mr. and Mrs. Smith. You and smiling Mr. and Mrs. Jones. Put all the pictures in a photo album in your lobby. Get approval from each client to put their picture in your Client Photo Album and then list their name beneath each picture. When a prospect comes in and is waiting to see you, they will have the opportunity to page through and see all the happy clients you work with. Chances are, the reason they are in your lobby in the first place is due to the lack of communication and service they are receiving from their current advisor. A picture says volumes about how satisfied and delighted your clients are and how different you are.

28

References Are Powerful.

The next time a client tells you how satisfied they are with your services, take the opportunity to find out if they would consider being a reference for you. Ask them if they would be willing to talk to a prospective client, every once in a while, if that prospective client wanted to know more about what it's like working with your firm.

If the client gives you the OK - add them to a list of client references. Code your references by the niche they may be in (retired from a particular company) or client type (similar age or demographics).

Print off a list of appropriate references for each prospective client. Oftentimes your prospective clients won't even call your references, but the fact that you have listed them shows your confidence in your firm's offerings and services.

(Remember to check with your compliance officer before using testimonials.)

29

Become The (Event) Host With The Most.

Marshall Field, the legendary retailing genius, once said that "Goodwill is the one and only asset that competition cannot undersell or destroy." One of the most effective ways to build that goodwill is to help others, by sharing your knowledge and expertise with them.

As a financial advisor, you have *a lot* of knowledge and expertise to share. Your method is simple: hold an event. What kind of event? The options are many and myriad. Imagine hosting free educational workshops and seminars with titles like these:

"Muzzling Uncle Sam: How to Keep Him from Taking Such a Big Tax Bite."

"Planning For The High Cost of Kids: From Playrooms To Ph.Ds."

"The Rules of Retirement Have Changed."

Of course, you don't have to hold your own seminars. You can sponsor community festivals or speak at your local Rotary Club or give a presentation at a trade show. The more you appear in front of the public, and the more prospects you attract, the more credibility you gain. And believe me—credibility is great for your business!

30

If You're Not, You Should Be!

If you aren't currently doing seminars, you should be! If you are, how can you make them more successful? Well, just keep on reading!

One of the challenges with seminars is getting qualified attendees to show up. For generating the highest number of attendees at your seminar, use proven sources. One proven source is Response Mail Express/Seminar Success (www.seminarsuccess.com). Their system absolutely gets lots of people to seminars. The rest is up to you!

Another strategy is to offer a very targeted seminar (NOT, for example, "General Investing for Every Investor"), mail it to a targeted list, and provide a targeted message filled with potential solutions. A good example: "Unlocking Your Retirement Funds," presented for individuals that are getting close to retirement from a specific company.

Tip-Within-A-Tip: Use the 5-5-5-20 Strategy.

Mail 5 invitations each to 5 people you know who work or worked at a target company. Ask them to pass the invitations to people they know who are getting ready to retire from that company. Then, follow up with a phone call to your 5 contacts. You may think it a miracle - but I have seen this simple strategy produce 20 qualified attendees consistently at seminars. Hence, 5-5-5-20!

31

Benefits, Benefits, Benefits.

In your financial seminars, are you selling products or selling solutions? Selling features or benefits? Giving all your solutions away or leaving some for a meeting after the seminar?

Seminar attendees are there because they are looking for solutions to what ails them. They are looking to see if you have the solutions for them and to determine, at least subconsciously, if you are trustworthy, experienced and knowledgeable.

Tell stories of success. Lay out problems and then describe possible solutions. You are selling concepts and the information that you have. But don't give it *all* away. Make sure there are enough incentives for the attendee to want to schedule an appointment with you to find out more.

Consider selling concepts and solutions while selling the benefits of working with you. Nothing else. A product seminar will never sell on an emotional level like a concept seminar will. A "concept sale" could be protecting and preserving assets and incomes, planning for the future, allocation, estate planning, charitable giving, real estate investing and alternatives, 401(k) rollover process, etc.

32

Leverage Your Events
To Create A Buzz.

You can't hold your event in a vacuum! Press releases, ads and invitations will get people there and create a buzz.

The more creative you can be with your event, the more "buzzworthy" it becomes. For instance, collect money, food or toys for charity at your seminar and commit that your firm will match whatever amount is collected. Or, have a local police officer come and speak at your Identity Theft Presentation.

Voila! You have a great hook for your press releases, ads, and invitations. With creative and goodwill-inspiring ideas, the local newspaper may well show up or cover your event. And, your name becomes even better known throughout the community.

33

Build Loyalty Through Client Appreciation Events.

The events we've just discussed are (or should be) open to the public. But there's another kind of event you should at least consider. Rather than all-inclusive, it's exclusive. That's right. I'm talking about a client appreciation event.

Why not host a picnic for your best clients, or a dinner, or even a workshop where you thank them? Alternately, you could hold a client orientation for your new clients, the ones you've just acquired in the previous quarter. This gives them an opportunity to ask questions, get to know your staff, find out more about your products and services, network with other clients and have fun.

Making your clients feel special is important, and holding an event that's open only to them is a surefire way to do that. The more special they feel, the more *loyal* they will be. And in an age where loyalty is sometimes non-existent, that's a valuable feeling indeed.

34

A Final Word About Events: Persistence, Not The Hard Sell, Pays Off.

"If you want to get your parking validated, you must sign up for an appointment tonight!" Come on. This or any other hard sell approach leads to canceled appointments and a loss of goodwill. Ok, so you won't do this to those that attend your seminar...

Sure, your ultimate hope is to sign up new clients. I know it, you know it, and the people who attend your seminars know it. Ask them politely to schedule an appointment tonight if they would like more information on the topics discussed - better yet, include an evaluation form that gives them a couple options of available appointment times in the coming week(s). Tell them you will follow up via phone tomorrow. If you can get through the presentation without resorting to aggressive tactics, you'll go a long way toward sustaining the goodwill you've generated with your event.

And if attendees are not ready to schedule an immediate appointment - don't give up so quickly! Once they have attended your seminar, they have learned some valuable information about you and your firm. However, they may not be ready immediately to do business with you. Keep in touch with attendees through systematic prospect marketing. Check out companies like www.KeepOnProspecting.com. They have developed a turn-key, easy, and inexpensive program consisting of mailing, emailing and calling attendees that will make the most of each seminar and bring in sales after the event. And, they do the work!

High-pressure sales tactics will result in cancellations and lost time and money. Persistence will pay off!

35

Direct Mail Works.

Want to hear something fascinating? Direct mail may be the oldest marketing tool on the planet. According to a spokesman for the New York University Center for Direct Marketing, "The roots of direct mail go back thousands of years and include messages written in hieroglyphics on papyrus and fabric sent throughout the Egyptian kingdom about 3000 B.C."

The next time you complain about the junk mail piling up on your kitchen counter, just realize that consumers have been dealing with the same phenomenon for at least five thousand years!

Which brings me to my point: direct mail works. Why else would so many companies spend so much money on it? Chances are, it will work for you, too—if you do it right. The next six tips cover the six "rights" of direct mail. Follow them to the letter and you'll see firsthand why those old Egyptians had the right idea.

36

Direct Mail Right #1:
The Right Design.

(See Tip #17 on Brochures.)

If you're thinking of inserting your brochure in an envelope, sticking a label on it and sending it off, stop right there. This approach will yield nothing but a big postage bill. If it looks like junk mail to you, it will look like junk mail to the recipient. Guess where your direct mail piece will end up?

You <u>must</u> do everything you can to make your direct mail piece look like a one-on-one communication—or at least, make it so intriguing that your client (or potential client) will want to open it. Here are a few tips:

- Don't use address labels. This screams "junk mail."
- If you have time—especially if you're inviting clients to a special event—ask someone with neat handwriting to address the envelopes. You may even try calligraphy.
- Hand-stamp your envelope…again, it looks more personal.
- Pique curiosity by using odd-size envelopes or packaging. Or put a creative headline on the envelope to entice the reader to open it and read on.
- Consider using a large postcard. That way, there's nothing to open and your message is right in front of the reader.

37

Direct Mail Right #2: The Right Message.

Every word you write must show the reader WIIFM…what's in it for me. He doesn't care that your firm is offering a new mutual fund. He <u>does</u> care that it can help him generate enough cash to take that month-long tour of Europe when he retires! Tout benefits, not features.

Also, you should include a special offer. Give readers something to respond to immediately. For example, offer a free retirement analysis. Invite them to RSVP to an event. Enclose a coupon good for a discount on a financial plan if used within 30 days (it's always a good idea to establish deadlines).

Make sure your direct mail piece is well-written and compelling. Provide as much information as you can. Surprising as it sounds, a one-page letter is not better than a three-page letter. Brevity may be the soul of wit, but it isn't the soul of direct mail!

Finally, if you are not a good writer, hire a professional. Just ask around…a trusted colleague is sure to know someone who can do a bang-up job with your direct mail piece.

38

Direct Mail Right #3:
The Right Markets.

Perhaps you want to target existing clients with your direct mail campaign. Not a bad idea. Marketing to clients is, after all, a cornerstone of *Red Zone Marketing*. But if you feel inclined to expand beyond your current clients, pick a list carefully. It's all too easy to end up with names outside your target market.

Use a list company with a reputation for delivering accurate lists that can be sorted based on the targeting information that's important to you. If you're clueless about list companies, visit www.InfoUSA.com…they're a good starting point.

You can target based on specific incomes, net worth, specific hobbies or interests, married people, single people, people with children, grandparents and more. The possibilities are numerous—just choose a list that meshes with your goals for your firm.

39

Direct Mail Right #4:
The Right Strategy.

Okay, you've bought your list. Let's say it has 10,000 names on it. You don't want to immediately send out the same direct mail package to every single name. That could be expensive and you might be very disappointed in the results.

Instead, select 1,000 or 1,500 names at random and mail to them. Better yet, send different offers to different segments of your list. By testing various combinations of names and offers, you can determine which package and which offer are most effective.

Testing is one of the great benefits of direct mail. When you buy a newspaper ad, it's impossible to know who saw it. But with direct mail, you know with reasonable certainty how many people got which message and what, if anything, they did about it. And this knowledge will serve you well in the future.

40

Direct Mail Right #5:
The Right Timing.

If you're going to use direct mail, go all out. Plan and maintain a regular schedule of mailings. I advise businesses to mail to <u>current</u> <u>clients</u> each month, or every six weeks at the minimum. Don't worry, this does not have to break the bank. Sometimes a simple postcard will maintain "top of mind" awareness.

You may be wondering if you really have this much to say to your clients. Sure you do! If you don't have a seminar coming up to invite them to, send a "Did You Know" piece about all of your offerings. Or send out a reprint of the latest newspaper story about your firm. If April 15th is fast approaching, send out tax tips. If Thanksgiving is just around the corner, send a Happy Turkey Day card.

What you're really doing is establishing a "Keeping in Touch (KIT) program—which I'll talk about later. Suffice it to say that the more timely, helpful information you send, the better. Direct mail is a great reinforcer of client relationships.

41

Direct Mail Right #6:
The Right Stuff.

Trying to conduct a successful marketing campaign without using direct mail is like trying to win a football game with your best players sitting on the bench. Neither will get you anywhere close to the *Red Zone*. But what if you don't have the ability or experience to produce direct mail?

First of all, even without experience you probably *do* have the ability. If not you, then *someone* in your firm. According to former U.S. Postmaster General William F. Bolger, "Direct mail…is a medium that many people use without the aid of outside help. It's a medium that can produce significant results even on a do-it-yourself basis." So with these encouraging words, use the advice I've just offered and take a stab at it.

If you're certain you don't have the wherewithal to produce effective direct mail, there are many firms that specialize in this type of marketing. And if you can't afford a firm, there are plenty of freelancers out there that can write letters and design postcards without charging you an exorbitant fee. Direct mail is just too important to ignore.

42

And Now, A Few Direct Mail "Wrongs."

Do not, I repeat, *do not* fall prey to these mistakes:

- Forgetting Your Digits. You design the perfect direct mail piece, but forget to include contact information or a response device. Duh! Actually, this is a more common mistake than you may realize. Always make it easy for the recipient to respond by providing your 800 number or including a postage-paid business reply envelope.
- All-Out Blitz. I mentioned this in Tip # 39, but it's worth reiterating. If you buy a large list (say, 10,000 names), sending the same packet to all of them at the same time is probably a waste of time and money. Don't do it.
- Tipping Your Hand. Window envelopes, pre-printed address labels and bulk postage permits all shout "Junk Mail!" and will probably wind up in the recipient's trash can—unopened. Review the design ideas in Tip #36.

43

Bone Up On Branding.

I'm sure you've heard about branding. But maybe you're not clear on exactly what it means. Perhaps this quote from Dr. David Aakers, a leading thinker in the field, will help: "[Branding is] the internalized sum of all impressions received by a consumer, which results in a distinctive position in their minds based on perceived emotional and functional benefits.'

In other words, every bit of communication your client receives—from the way you answer your telephone to your corporate logo to the direct mail package you send out—contributes to your brand.

What brand are you building for your company? Creating the right image for your business is critical to your success. Remember, there are hundreds of thousands of financial advisors in the U.S. Your brand should set you apart from—actually above—the crowd.

Uncover Your USP.

If the last tip gave you a slightly panicky feeling, don't worry. Many companies don't have a clearly defined brand, or at least don't communicate it to the world. In other words, you're not alone. But you *are* in a precarious position—teetering on the edge of the cliff overlooking commodityville—so you need to find some solid ground, and fast.

What is your Unique Selling Proposition, or USP? What is different about your company that you could promote in an effort to brand your offering in the client's mind? What sets you apart from the crowd? Your USP should state your main benefit to consumers, solicit an emotional response, and appeal to your target audience. It should be memorable.

Put it on all of your marketing materials, letterhead, business cards, signage, media material, folders and forms to project and reinforce the same image.

Take a "time out" right now and pinpoint your USP.

45

What's In A Name...
Namely, Yours?

Take a look at the business listings in the white pages of your local telephone directory. Do you see lots of names like The Morgan Company, Brown & Associates, Smith & Green, The Anderson Group? Notice that these names say nothing about what they do and who their customers might be.

Now, I realize that financial advisors tend to be, by nature, somewhat traditional. That means many of you—note I didn't say *all*—are inclined to adopt names along the lines of the ones I listed above. But while you're thinking about brands and USPs and all that good stuff, you might want to consider your company name. Does it convey who you are and what makes you different?

Now, I'm not suggesting that you adopt a lowbrow name like "Investments R Us." But, just for the sake of argument, let's say your USP is that you help clients integrate charitable giving strategies into their overall money management plans. Couldn't you call yourself something like, say, The Caring Investment Group, Inc? It immediately conveys what makes you different.

It's something to think about.

46

Invest In A Good Looking Logo.

Emblazon this advice on your bathroom mirror, if need be: *unless you are trained in graphic design, <u>do</u> <u>not</u> attempt to create your own logo!*

Forget the fact that you used to draw a lot in elementary school. Banish the thought that a sketch of your kitty, Mr. Whiskers, would look awfully cute on your letterhead. Resist the all-too-tempting idea that a logo design contest would give your employees a chance to express their creativity.

Hire a design firm or a reputable freelance designer. Explain to this agency or individual what your company is all about, what makes you different, who your audience is. Then, let them (or him or her) take the reins. Your company logo is too important <u>not</u> to place in the competent hands of professionals.

47

Test and Track Your Advertising.

Did you know the average American is subjected to more than 3,000 marketing messages daily? That's a lot of advertising. You can see why it's a big challenge for one little financial services agency to stand out from the competition.

All of which leads up to my next piece of advice: test your advertising. Test your headline, your message, your ad size. As advertising executive David M. Ogilvy said, "The most important word in the vocabulary of advertising is TEST. If you pre-test your product with consumers, and pre-test your advertising, you will do very well in the marketplace."

I would add that TRACK is the *second* most important word. If you track where your business is coming from, you can determine what advertising media are working for you. Purchase an 800 number, or use a different number in each of your ads. Or simply ask clients how they heard about you and track your findings.

Once you know what kinds of ads work for you—and which media reach your target audience—you can make effective decisions that will keep your ads head and shoulders above your 3,000 competitors.

48

Want Local Clients?
Newspaper's A Natural!

If yours is the kind of financial service agency that targets clients based in your geographic area, newspaper advertising is quite successful.

Check each paper's circulation before making a decision. A paid-circulation paper will typically generate more sales, because readers have invited the medium into their homes. I.e., your ad is likely to be seen.

However, free newspapers can also offer success. Just remember the magic words, *test* and *track*. Same goes for weekly vs. daily circulation.

Of course, if your clients tend to be dispersed all over the country, newspaper advertising is probably not for you…but you already knew that.

49

Don't Forget The Humble Yellow Pages.

I'll admit that there may not be a huge number of wealthy individuals who find their financial planners by flipping through the Yellow Pages—but you never know.

Imagine this scenario: a few miles away lives an eccentric octogenarian who decides that maybe it's *not* a good idea to leave her millions to her 27 cats. Maybe, she thinks, it's time to do some estate planning. She pulls out her phone book, looks in the Yellow Pages (where you aren't listed)…and calls your biggest competitor. Yikes!

To avoid such a fate—and to make things easier for local clients who've lost your business card—you should have an ad in the Yellow Pages. It goes without saying that your ad should stand apart from the competition. One proven strategy is to use a white background. Another is to buy a larger ad—they're selected three times more often than their smaller counterparts. (I guess size *does* matter, at least in the Yellow Pages.)

50

Consider Cable.

Unless you are one of the huge investment firms—it's unlikely that you can afford a TV spot on the three major networks. But cable spots...ah, that's a horse of a different color!

Local cable systems are able to preempt the spots feeding down from the network satellites and fill them with local spots. These locally available spots, or "avails," offer advertisers a much narrower geographic distribution at a lower cost.

So determine exactly whom you're trying to reach with your commercials (say, affluent single women over 55). Look at the demographic data for your clients. Then match the cable network programming to your target, and schedule your commercials when your target audience is watching TV (say, during that mid-afternoon gardening show). Pretty simple, huh?

51

Reach 'Em On The Radio.

You may never have considered advertising on the radio. That's okay. For most small businesses, it is definitely the road less traveled. But with more than 23 million people listening to local community radio and new stations launching all the time, more and more businesses are realizing the power of on-air advertising.

Radio ads can be created very cost efficiently, a boon for the smaller financial services firm. Radio stations usually offer in-house creative and production services at fairly affordable rates. (Of course, if you're a larger company you should let your ad agency take the radio ad from concept to recording.)

Just be sure you pick the right station or stations to advertise on. Get demographic statistics and make sure your target audience will be listening during the time period your spot is broadcast.

And be sure to determine a frequency of advertising that will bring you results. Ideally, you should get your message across at least three times in a "purchase cycle." The first time will provide recognition, the next time will compel the listener to pay attention, and the final time will solicit action.

52

Make The Most of Magazine Advertising.

Why are magazines such an effective advertising medium? Because the folks who read specific magazines—both trade and consumer—tend to fall into fairly predictable categories. Picture the typical reader for publications centered on hunting & fishing…fine wines…doll collecting…heavy metal music. Four very distinct and different images come to mind, don't they?

As a financial advisor, you probably know (or can guess) what magazines your target audience reads. If you want to sell estate planning services to affluent seniors, you'd never take out an ad in a publication titled, oh, let's say, *Teenybopper World*. You might consider lifestyle, travel or finance magazines instead.

Of course, you can probably expect to pay a hefty ad rate for the better-known magazines with larger circulation numbers. But that's only fair. You're getting a lot of bang for your ad buck.

53

Strategic Alliances: Working Together Works.

Ponder this 1998 quote from Brian F. O'Connell, director of strategic partnership development at Inderdev, Seattle, Washington: "In the business world, radically changing socio-economic realities, along with the demand for a higher return on investment, led to the acknowledgment long ago that…strategic alliances and partnerships have now turned former competitors into new collaborators."

Phrased another way, two heads are better than one.

A strategic alliance takes place when two separate businesses work together to offer a broader set of skills or services to joint clients, to the mutual benefit of both parties. Both companies thus create an advantage over competitors by broadening the scope of their operations.

Make sure you get a commitment from your alliance partner that the referral will go both ways. And, don't be afraid to walk away quickly if you don't find it an equitable arrangement.

So, can you think of a company with which you might join forces, either formally or informally? If not, don't worry. The next two tips will clarify what I mean and perhaps spark some ideas for you.

54

Connect With A Company In A Similar Industry.

Let's say that your financial planning firm is located right next door to a law office or accounting firm. Why not forge a strategic alliance partnership so you all can enjoy a steady stream of referrals and new business?

Unfortunately, however, many strategic alliances are one way relationships where you refer your clients to the other firm but they don't return the favor. Why? Perhaps you need to strengthen the relationship with the strategic alliance. The other professional won't refer their clients to you if they feel even a hint of uncertainty about you or your firm. Every month, schedule a lunch with your alliances (even after they have begun to refer business to you). Share with these alliances, through stories, information about clients you have helped (without sharing confidential information, of course) and the services you provide. Ask them about their business. When you increase their confidence in you and strengthen that relationship, you may be surprised at how referrals will begin making their way to you.

55

Join Forces With A Partner in a Different Industry.

Unless Ebenezer Scrooge patronizes your firm, most of your clients don't live for the joy of poring over financial statements and counting the money you help them invest. They *do* have other outside needs and interests. That's why it can pay to team up with a company in a totally different industry, as long as that company serves the same market as you.

Let's say your specialty is offering financial advice to families who are concerned about saving for their kids' college educations. Obviously, these families should start saving right away, so you need to catch them when their children are small. You decide to team up with Dayna's Daycare Center.

You can work out a deal whereby Dayna invites her customers (the parents, not the children!) to attend an exclusive financial planning seminar hosted by none other than you. In return, you hand out brochures to your clients about her daycare center (along with glowing verbal recommendations).

You can see how both you and Dayna could get lots of great leads from this arrangement. Such strategic alliances are practically painless, and all they require is a dash of ingenuity and a pinch of cooperation.

56

Serve Your Community (But Not In A Self-Serving Way).

What you give is what you get! This seems to be a law of the universe. And it's as true in marketing as in every other area of life.

When you and your company give back to your community—volunteering time, raising funds for non-profit organizations, spearheading local initiatives—you become a truly valued member of that community. And the rewards of being an active, committed and valued community member come back to you again and again in the form of business and support. This is a powerful form of marketing.

Just don't let marketing be your primary motive for local involvement. Joining a service club, charitable group or civic organization for prospecting reasons will backfire on you. Self-serving motives fool no one. Get involved to serve—and serve willingly and cheerfully—and you will be rewarded...both personally and professionally.

57

Find Your Natural Niche...

Did you know the word "niche" is derived from the French *se nicher*, which is translated as "to build a nest?" Finding your niche in the business world is exactly that: building your nest.

To maximize your chances of success you must focus on a particular corner of the financial marketplace, rather than trying to be all things to all people. If you already know what your niche is, great! You're ahead of the game. If you don't, just look at your current clients and pinpoint the ones you most enjoy doing business with, or the ones that are most lucrative.

As a financial advisor, you have many potential niches. People that have retired from the same company, divorced women...soon-to-be retirees...middle-class families...small business owners...upwardly mobile thirty-something professionals...self-employed folks or entrepreneurs...mega-corporations...pro athletes.

Once you know your niche, you'll be able to use your time more effectively and efficiently and you'll automatically set yourself up for a stream of qualified referrals. Which brings me to my next tip...

58

...And Get Entrenched.

Okay, you've found your natural niche. Your mission now is to dig in and hold on. With everything you do, you must position yourself firmly in your niche market.

Take a cue from Mountain Dew. Everything PepsiCo does to market this soft drink focuses on young, high-energy, adventure-seeking individuals. It doesn't pretend to be a favorite of the conservative 50-something crowd. You should do the same.

The next four tips will give you some ideas on how to entrench yourself deeply into your chosen niche.

59

Join A Trade Association.

Become an expert in the industry you've decided to focus on. Start by going to the library and researching all the associations that are out there. Or search online at the American Association of Association Executives (yes, that's a real organization!)

Pick one or two associations where you feel you can make a contribution and attend a few of their meetings. Join one of them to get you started and *voila!*—you've gained access.

But don't simply join. Get involved. Your active participation will help you build your niche. Remember: people do business with people they know—with people they like—and with people they trust.

60

Write For Industry Publications.

Anywhere from 50 to 80 percent of articles in newspapers and trade journals are generated from press releases and publicity. What does this statistic mean to you? Basically, it means you don't have to be an employee of a magazine to get an article published within its pages.

Trade journals are often on the lookout for well-written articles focusing on areas of interest to their readers. Submit one or two good ones and the editors may keep coming back to you for more. That kind of exposure quickly positions you as an expert in your field, increasing your likelihood of attracting prospective clients.

By the way, if you don't feel comfortable writing an article in your area of expertise, you can hire a professional wordsmith to do it for you. Don't worry, your name will still go on the article—and your firm will still get the "expert" status!

61

Host A Niche Seminar.

You can create opportunities to cultivate your niche. For instance, consider doing seminars for a particular segment of the marketplace. Small business associations, chambers of commerce, and other organizations host periodic "brown bag" lunches or breakfast meetings and are often looking for speakers.

Check the calendar section of your local newspaper to see which organizations do these kinds of programs and then contact them. You probably won't get any fees, but it's a great way to solidify your position in a particular niche and develop a stream of prospects.

By the way, don't overlook individual companies, many of which regularly bring in outsiders to conduct training seminars or educational workshops for their staff members. Do a good job the first time, and you may be invited back often. If you can't get into the company, perhaps you can gain entrÈe through the union or an association they belong to and do seminars, presentations or educational workshops for them.

62

Become A Sponsor.

Sponsorships offer excellent opportunities for you to gain significant added exposure for your financial advising services. Just think creatively.

If your niche is new parents, buy a booth at the "Baby Fair" held at your local hospital.

If your niche is the over-fifty crowd, sponsor the "Senior Dance" held at your local community center.

If your niche consists of the employees of a large corporation, sponsor its bowling or softball team or underwrite the cost of its newsletter.

In the words of Walt Kelly's cartoon character Pogo, "We're surrounded by insurmountable opportunities." Pick out a couple and go ahead and surmount them!

63

You Must Create A
Client Experience.

This is a major cornerstone of the *Red Zone Marketing* philosophy.

It's no longer enough to fulfill your clients' basic needs. To avoid becoming a commodity, you must go beyond satisfying them. You must <u>delight</u> them. In the words of B. Joseph Pine II and James H. Gilmore—authors of *The Experience Economy: Work Is Theatre & Every Business A Stage* (Harvard Business School Press, 1999)—"you must learn to stage a rich, compelling experience."

If you aren't absolutely delighting your clients, they will go elsewhere. They may even tell others of their dissatisfaction. In most cases, they won't even tell you they're dissatisfied. In fact, for each one who does complain to you, there are nine others who'll complain to everyone but you and then possibly disappear without bothering to tell you why.

But <u>how</u> do I delight my clients? you're probably wondering. *<u>How</u> do I stage a rich, compelling experience?* Read on! The following eight or so tips will give you some ideas to chew on.

64

Call And Ask 'Em How You're Doing.

Do your best clients call *you* or do *you* call them? The truth is, the more they initiate contact with you, the less satisfied they're likely to be. If you've been hearing a lot more rings than dial tones lately, it's time to do a bit of field research.

Right now, make a list of your ten best clients. Then, call each one of them to see how they're doing and more important, how *you* are doing. Are they completely satisfied with your services? If not, why not? What could you do better?

Of course you should listen to the answers you get. But just the fact that you're calling at all means you've won half the battle. It lets your star clients know how important they are to you…and everyone needs to feel important!

65

Ponder The Power of Client Marketing.

By now you're probably getting the picture that marketing to clients may even be more important than marketing to cold prospects. You are right. It costs ten times more in time and effort to get a new client than it does to retain a current one. So if you are focusing your marketing efforts on prospects, I urge you to rethink your approach.

Need a little more convincing? Let me tell you a story: I have a client who has been a financial advisor for more than a dozen years. During his first eight years in business (before he became a *Red Zone Marketer*) he had accumulated $10 million in money under management. He was acquiring more than 80 percent of his new clients by prospect marketing—seminars, direct mail, advertising and networking.

When we began working together, I advised him to add client marketing to the mix. We put together a system that included regular phone calls and mail communications to his clients, client focused seminars and events, open houses, a commitment to periodic client reviews and ongoing client appreciation activities.

Within three years after putting this plan in place, his business increased from $10 million to $100 million under management. In only three years! And by the end of the fifth year, he had $200 million under management. Wouldn't *you* like to be a similar success story? Let your clients help you.

66

Estimate The Lifetime Value Of Your Clients.

Do you think of each new client acquired as a one-time "victory?" If so, you may want to start thinking longer term. What is the lifetime value of a client? Once you've determined this, you may find a new inspiration for servicing and communicating with clients.

Estimating the lifetime value of a client can be a real eye-opener. For instance, a Taco Bell customer isn't merely someone who walks in today and spends three or four dollars on lunch. Taco Bell has estimated that the lifetime value of that customer is an amazing $12,000! That's a whole lot of burritos, amigo! For automobile manufacturers, the lifetime value of a customer averages $340,000.

To calculate the lifetime value of your clients, you'll need to take into account the fees or commissions generated. You also may want to take into account their referrals, and the revenue they will generate. This exercise will tell you clearly which clients mean the most to your business.

If nothing else, you may never take a client for granted again!

67

Make Yourself Memorable (Memorability, Part I)

Refer back to Tip #63 for a moment. Do you feel that your financial services firm is in danger of becoming a commodity? If your answer is *yes*, you'd better consider how you can become part of the Experience Economy. Experiences engage individuals in a personal way. Experiences are memorable, and will keep clients coming back for more.

I have two financial advisor clients who have gotten very good at creating memorable experiences for *their* clients. One of them is very health conscious. He incorporates healthful food, videos, books, posters and seminars into his business offerings. He's providing an experience—a total healthy life plan that focuses on his clients' overall wellbeing.

Another client has created "The Life Enjoyment Experience™," the idea being that he helps his clients "get to the top of the mountain." From the mountaintop you can see and experience the enjoyment of the world—so he has designed six conference rooms in his office to represent a different city of the world. One room has a huge mural of London on the wall; another one represents San Francisco and so on. He reports that people bring their friends by to see his unique facilities, even without an appointment. Can you imagine a better way to attract new business?

68

Give 'Em Something To Talk About! (Memorability, Part II)

In the last tip I gave you a couple of examples of financial services firms that work to create memorable client experiences. Now, I want to approach the same point from a slightly different angle: the reason such tactics work is because, to borrow a phrase from songstress Bonnie Raitt, they give clients "something to talk about."

When clients want to talk about the experiences they have with your business (assuming it's *positive* talk, of course!), it means you're doing something right. And it means they're much more likely to refer their friends and colleagues to you. (I'll be covering the critical issue of referrals very shortly.)

So what are you giving your clients to talk about? If you suspect they're not talking, you'd better change that! Make a list of the possible "experiences" you could offer your clients. You may want to brainstorm ideas with your colleagues. And keep in mind, although "giving them something to talk about" is serious, dollars & cents business, it can also be a lot of fun!

69

Create A Client Delight KIT Program.

I've already mentioned the phenomenon of the "Keep In Touch" (or KIT) Program. (See Tip #25.) It is an important element in creating memorable client experiences. Establishing a KIT Program—which centers on regular, value-added communications with your clients—is not something you do "off the cuff." It takes PLANNING, EFFORT and COMMITMENT.

Determine a year in advance how you want to communicate with your clients each month. You'll probably use phone calls, e-mails, snail-mail and maybe even the occasional in-person visit to accomplish your goal. KIT communications can be anything from a birthday card to a casual e-mail about a new service you're offering to a personal phone call inviting them to a client appreciation dinner.

The point is to cement client relationships by making proactive contact on a regular basis. Your **clients** will be delighted by this regularly occurring evidence that you truly <u>do</u> value their business. I've said it before and I'll say it again: <u>everyone</u> needs to feel needed and appreciated. The more your clients hear from you, the better your business relationship is likely to be.

70

Take the Headache Out of Your Follow-Up and Client Contact.

If you are committed to communicating regularly with your prospects and clients but you're not sure how in the world you're going to get it done, consider investing in a contact management software program.

True relationship management software can be a real lifesaver for people in the financial services industry. For instance, Advisors Assistant (www.climark.com) and Practice Builder (www.financialsoftware.com) are used by many financial advisors and insurance agents. These programs will allow you to create a Client Delight Program to target and communicate through use of a foolproof system of client activity management, letters, scheduled follow-ups and sequences.

Each client and prospect should have an activity scheduled in the database. If they don't, then ask yourself why they are in your database. Great, hassle-free follow-up will bring in all kinds of good things to your business including more business, referrals and (did I mention?)...more business!

71

Schedule Regular Phone Appointments With Your Top Clients.

Several times a year you should schedule regular phone appointments with your best clients. These contacts are in a whole different category from the five-minute "Just calling to say Happy Holidays" calls that might appear on your regular KIT Program schedule. They are much more in-depth and intense.

The purpose of such calls? Well, part of it is to find out what kind of job you're doing. Mostly, though, you should use these calls to find out what's going on in your clients' lives and brainstorm ways you can help them.

For instance, if a client just welcomed a new grandchild into the world, you might suggest he start a college savings plan to supplement the little one's future education. It may or may not dramatically increase revenues immediately, but it will lead directly to a more delighted client, referrals and all of their business.

There's just one caveat: if you get the feeling that a client considers your call a pushy, obnoxious invasion of her privacy, back off fast. Respect the client and your good intentions won't backfire.

72

An Educated Client
Is A Happy Client.

A big part of your KIT Program should involve educating your clients. Just contacting them every month isn't enough; you must make sure the communications are meaningful.

As a financial advisor, you've forgotten more about money management than your clients will know in a lifetime. So use that knowledge to your advantage! Video or audiotape educational seminars and mail copies to clients who didn't attend. Send "FYI" e-mails about any new products or services your firm may offer. Regularly mail them an info-packed organization newsletter (see Tips 13-16).

You may even consider setting up a recorded weekly update that clients can call into regarding new offerings from your firm and/or timely industry issues. Finally, when a client asks a question, give a thorough, detailed answer and make sure she understands. (I.e., *don't* take a patronizing "Don't worry your pretty little head about that; just let me handle it!" approach.)

Your clients view you as a dependable source of useful information, a source they can tap anytime they desire. Proactively showing them that you *want* to educate them is the path to achieving this goal.

73

Get Your Whole Team On The Same Game Plan.

All of *your* efforts at creating great client experiences and "Keeping In Touch" will be for naught if someone else in your company drops the ball. If someone implementing your marketing faithfully contacts a client or prospect every month, but client service representatives consistently misspell a name, get the address wrong, or fail to follow up on a request or complaint, the entire company suffers the consequences.

That's why, before you implement any of the strategies discussed in this book, you need to sit down with your entire team and explain why you're doing what you're doing—and why everyone must be following the same game plan. Your clients are their clients, your failure is their failure, your win is their win. That's how it works in sports...and in the business world.

74

Don't Abandon The Running Game.

In football, when the star running back fumbles the ball, the coach doesn't wail "That's it! We're <u>never</u> going to run the ball again!" That would be absurd, right. And it's equally absurd to try a marketing tactic only once—seminar marketing, for instance—and give up just because you got lackluster results.

Not every play in football is successful every time, and neither is every tactic in marketing. If you believe seminar marketing works—and clearly it does, judging by the successful advisors using this strategy year after year—don't give up on it after one disappointing try. Realize that something must have been wrong in your strategy or your implementation and figure out how to do it better.

As the old saying goes, if at first you don't succeed, try, try again!

75

Find Opportunities In Obstacles.

A big part of being a *Red Zone Marketer* is having an optimistic outlook and figuring out how to turn the stumbling blocks you encounter into stepping stones.

Let me tell you a story about a colleague of mine. During his tenure as director of marketing at a local bank, disaster struck. For months, he had been promoting what was to be the bank's second branch office. Then, just a few days before the grand opening, a fire destroyed the building.

What did my friend do? Well, even before the blaze was extinguished, he had a photographer on hand taking pictures of the burning structure. He then turned them into newspaper ads with copy like "Sorry You Missed Our Housewarming—It Wasn't Quite The Way We Planned It!" Later ads showed construction of the new office in progress, proclaiming, "You Can Build—While We Rebuild," and encouraging readers to use the bank's temporary facilities next door.

A year later the bank *finally* staged its grand opening. The volunteer fire department, which had fought the blaze, displayed its equipment in the parking lot, and the traditional ribbon-cutting ceremony was replaced by—of course!—a ribbon burning.

The moral of my story is simple: whenever you face obstacles in your business (or in your life for that matter), look for ways to turn them into opportunities. It may take a bit of searching, but it can almost always be done.

76

Referrals Are The Backbone Of Successful Selling.

Throughout this book I have addressed the importance of focusing your marketing efforts on current clients, not cold prospects. That's not to say prospects should be ignored; obviously, *any* growth-oriented business needs a regular infusion of fresh blood. It's just that where those prospects come from makes all the difference in the world—and it's always best if they come through your current clients.

That's right. I'm talking about referrals. The clients you already have can and should be major players in helping you find new business. In fact, referrals from them are the best leads you can ever hope to receive. They are loyal, easy to close, cost-efficient, and likely to become a source of even *more* referrals!

And the best part is, if you're providing valuable, worthwhile services to your clients, they'll want to share you with others. It's one of the nicer aspects of human nature. All you have to do is give them a little nudge…and the next few tips will tell you how.

77

Create A Client Referral System.

The first step in creating a good client referral system is to change your mindset. Quit looking at referrals as something extra, a "doggie bone" that a client tosses you every once in a while. That mindset is wrong! Everything you do should be geared to receiving and following up on referrals.

In other words, take a systems-based approach. If you have a system in place for asking for and pursuing referrals—a system that has been communicated to your entire team—then you and your staff will use it. You won't have to think, "Now what information can I send to this referral?" or "How can I thank this client for giving me this referral?" You'll have a package on hand to instantly drop in the mail. It'll be as automatic as brushing your teeth.

Of the business owners I speak to across the country, 90 percent say they ask for referrals only occasionally. Why not be among the 10 percent that do it regularly and faithfully? In other words, it's time to work out your referral system. The next seven tips will provide some great suggestions to get you started.

78

Just ASK.

The best method for acquiring referrals is to simply ask. Ask all the time. Ask honestly, sincerely, and without shame. There's nothing wrong with asking clients and even prospects for names of people who might be interested in your financial planning services. Chances are, they will probably be glad to help you out.

Of course, *how* you ask does make a difference. There's an old pushy approach that involves putting a pad of paper in front of your client and waiting until he has written down five or ten names of friends and associates. Do not try this! Some clients may resent it, and some may resent it enough to never give you referrals.

It's much better to take a subtler approach. Ask open-ended questions—"What have you liked about the work we've done together?"—and when you get a positive response, follow up by asking "Is there anyone else you know who may need the same services you are benefitting from?" Or say, "My expertise is working with people like you who have a need for the financial services I provide. Who else do you know who may need my help?"

You'll be pleasantly surprised by the leads you'll get!

79

If You're Too Shy To Ask, Ask In Writing.

There are certain people who simply can't bring themselves to make a face-to-face request for referrals. Perhaps you are one of them. Hey, it's okay. Asking for anything can be psychologically uncomfortable—and fortunately, there is another option.

Send a referral request package to all of your clients. It should include a warm cover letter and a form on which the recipient can list friends and business associates who might be interested in your services. The form would include a space for names, addresses and phone numbers (both home and work), as well as a "Call this person and use my name" check box. Include a stamped, self-addressed business reply envelope to make it very easy for the recipient. (You might also include a FAX number and email for quicker response.)

Once you've created this package, you can drop it in the mail every time you acquire a new client. *Voila!* Your system is now in place!

80

Don't Discount Referrals From Surprising Places.

As surprising as it sounds, it is possible to get referrals from competitors, current prospects, and even former prospects.

Let's say you've provided valuable information to others who, for whatever reason, decided not to do business with you but still appreciate what you did for them. Why would they *not* refer business to you? Likewise, why wouldn't a competitor send a potential client your way if they were not the right "fit" for him but are perfect for you?

You can also get great referrals from members of churches, associations or special interest groups. And don't assume that your family members and friends know exactly what you do. (I can't tell you how many times I've heard from my loved ones, "Now *what* is it that you do again?") Your closest relatives are probably your biggest fans and can be wonderful referral sources. Put them on your mailing list…and clearly communicate to them what you do for a living!

81

Become A List Lord.

An association, industry, department, or club-membership list can open the door to referrals. For example, you may be having lunch with a member of the local Small Business Association. Just pull out the membership list and say, "I was wondering if you know any other members who may be interested in my financial planning services?" You'll be amazed at the response you get.

Why does the list method work? Quite simply, because people want to show that they have influence in the groups they belong to. Once they have identified some names, you can call these people and say, "Hello, I'm Betty Jones. Bill Smith, a fellow member of the Small Business Association, said you may be interested in the services that I offer." It's a great way to get more referrals without putting anyone on the spot.

82

Remember The "R" Word.

The biggest challenge in making referrals your top source of new business is creating a company-wide "referral mindset." Here's a suggestion that may help. Put a sign in your office with a big "R" printed on it. Every time you look at it you'll be reminded to "Remember Referrals." But the best part is this: it may also inspire clients (or even prospects!) to ask the meaning, which creates the perfect opening for you to explain that referrals are the heart of your business—and that you'd appreciate their help!

When you're not in your office, a lapel pin with an "R" on it will probably generate the same question, increasing your opportunities to ask for referrals.

Include the word "Referrals" on agendas you bring to every client/prospect meeting you have so that you won't forget this critical task. Colleagues and staff people should all agree to remind each other of the importance of the "R" word—this way, remembering referrals will quickly become an office-wide habit!

It may sound a bit hokey, but it actually works!

83

Persuade Your Clients With A Club.

No, I'm not suggesting any form of violence! I'm talking about launching a referral club, which will create a sense of belonging and encourage members to provide—you guessed it!—referrals.

You might consider hosting a referral-appreciation dinner that's open exclusively to club members and their referrals. Or you could partner with a local business, Sally's Tropical Fish Paradise or Dinah's Cajun Cookin' Shack, for example. When the referral-rewards club card is taken to Sally's or Dinah's, they will give your clients a 10 percent discount on any purchase. Or perhaps you could simply send club members a special mailing or newsletter.

There are many possibilities, actually. Whatever type of club you decide on, just be sure that it enhances your firm's image and promotes ongoing dialogue with your clients. It has to be a two-way street.

84

Say It With Flowers...
Or More Creative Rewards.

Saying "thank you" to clients who give you referrals encourages even *more* referrals. So each time you receive a referral, send that client a note and a nice gift. Flowers and gift baskets are time-tested winners. But you can also be a bit more innovative. For instance, give:

- A book on a subject you know they're interested in
- Homemade cookies or other treats (only if you can bake; otherwise, have Grandma do it!)
- Tickets to a sporting event, the theater, or the movies
- A spa gift certificate
- A free car wash or a fuel card ("practical" gifts are often the most appreciated ones of all and encourage more referring!).

Another tangible way to express your appreciation is make a donation to her favorite charity, or offer to sponsor his child's Little League team. Be creative—just be sure that you go above and beyond the call of duty to say "thank you" for providing such a valuable and generous service.

85

Find Your Passion!

I saved this tip for last, because I believe it puts the exclamation point on every idea, suggestion and word of advice in this book. Without passion, every tip in this book is useless—or at least, greatly diminished in its power.

If, after trying out some new ideas—and really throwing yourself into them—you can't muster up any energy or enthusiasm for your work, you may have to face the fact that you are in the wrong field. But you know what? I doubt that will be the case. I've found that most people who approach every day with zest and zeal and a true passion for living are the way they are because they *decided* to be.

If you conclude that the world is a wonderful, fun place filled with excitement and opportunity, it <u>will</u> be. It's that simple.

A man named Fred Shero once commented, "Success is not the result of spontaneous combustion. You must first set yourself on fire." That's it exactly! That's the key to your success—passionately believing you can win. If you do have passion, then you'll find it easy to get up in the morning, overcome challenges, carve out a niche, ask for referrals, get that new business, and give your clients the extraordinary, outrageous kind of service and experience that will keep them on your team forever.

Now get out there and do it! That's the best way to move from the Red Zone to the End Zone more often!

Red Zone Marketing Products
and Services

Red Zone Marketing: A Playbook For Winning All The Business You Want

Is Your Company Competing In—And Scoring From—The Red Zone? *This Extraordinary Book Tells You How!* To find and keep new business, just ask Maribeth Kuzmeski, inspired marketer and lifelong sports fan. In this idea-filled book, she explains how to move your sales and marketing team into the *Red Zone*—the final 20 yards before the goal line, or in your case, the unmarked territory where you either win or lose a client—and how to SCORE once you get there.

Red Zone Marketing: A Playbook For Winning All The Business You Want (AUDIOBOOK - CD)

Is Your Company Competing In—And Scoring From—The Red Zone? *This Extraordinary AudioBook Tells You How!* To find and keep new business, just ask Maribeth Kuzmeski, inspired marketer and lifelong sports fan. In this idea-filled audiobook, she explains how to move your sales and marketing team into the *Red Zone*—the final 20 yards before the goal line, or in your case, the unmarked territory where you either win or lose a client—and how to SCORE once you get there.

Marketing Strategies for Extraordinary Sales (DVD)

Watch, listen and learn the playbook for winning more business! Join author Maribeth Kuzmeski in the Red Zone Marketing Locker-Room where she shares a wealth of techniques for finding and keeping new business. This DVD shows how to move your sales and marketing team down the field and into the Red Zone—the final 20 yards before the goal line, or in your case, the unmarked territory where you either win or lose a client—and how to SCORE once you get there.

This dynamic video is the digital version of the book, *Red Zone Marketing*. It is filled with the most successful, cost-effective and highest ROI marketing strategies that today's businesses use to stay on top. Use it with your staff, motivate yourself, and find unique ways to stay in front of the competition. A surefire touchdown for your business!

The Client Experience (Audio CD)

Want to eavesdrop on a brilliant game plan? Introducing an audio presentation by Maribeth Kuzmeski describing how to positively delight your clients. Listen to her key strategies for staging a rich, compelling and unexpected experience for your clients, so not only will they come back for more, they'll bring their friends. Before you know it, you'll be scoring from the red zone—again and again! We're calling audibles here!

Marketing Planning Guide

Take a time-out and plan your marketing today! The Marketing Planning Guide is a marketing plan template that will give you valuable direction and guidance for your marketing plan. When your strategy, calendar, timeline of activities and tools are clearly defined, that will inevitably lead to more success. This workbook will become your custom Marketing Plan for Client Delight and Success that you can implement immediately for results in your business! Take a time-out today and use this guide to plan your marketing!

The Client Delight® System

Investors continue to be "somewhat" to "not" satisfied with the amount of communication they receive from their financial advisor. Red Zone Marketing will guide you through creating a Client Delight® System for your company. Develop a system for communicating with your current clients that may include events, phone calls, mailings, reviews and meetings. The tested and proven Client Delight® System will generate referrals, additional business, long-term clients and - yes - is in the best interest of you - and your clients!

Referral System & Tools for Financial Advisors

Referral Systems & Tools for Financial Advisors explores the various ways financial advisors can use the power of referrals to dramatically increase their business. Discover a collection of specific and extraordinary referral-boosting strategies, systems, worksheets, scripts & talking points, referral letter templates, referral gaining forms, postcards, thank you letters and gift ideas... all ready to use on CD!

A Financial Planners Guide to Successful Client Appreciation Events

Learn the successful strategies for using client appreciation events to help build and secure your book of business. The combination of this booklet, PowerPoint presentation and 500 invitations and envelopes will give you all the tools to experience the benefits of adding client appreciation events to your annual marketing plan.

On-Site Consultation

Comprehensive on-site marketing consulting services include a full analysis of all marketing tools, strategies, implementation, staffing and business systems. Red Zone Marketing also will analyze marketing seminars and events and offer recommendations for improving the overall operations of the firm. Hundreds of on-site evaluations have already been done with remarkable Red Zone Marketing results!

Speaking Services

Learn the marketing, prospecting and Client Delight® strategies that have led advisors to enormous success. National keynote speaker, marketing consultant, author and personal coach, Maribeth Kuzmeski, has been working with and studying successful financial advisors for years. She personally consults some of the nation's top financial advisors, and, under her guidance one advisor built a business from $10 million to $200 million in money under management in five years. Attendees will leave with proven, tangible strategies they can put to work right away for more success and will have the motivation to do it!

To contact Maribeth Kuzmeski:

Red Zone Marketing
1509 N. Milwaukee Ave.
Libertyville, IL 60048
847-367-4066 phone
847-367-5226 fax
info@redzonemarketing.com
www.redzonemarketing.com

Sign up for our online tips
at www.redzonemarketing.com